CHICOPEE PUBLIC LIBR
449 Front Street
Chicopee, MA 01013

SO-BZE-926

Evan Williams, Biz Stone, Jack Dorsey, and

Twitter

INTERNET BIOGRAPHIES™

Evan Williams, Biz Stone, Jack Dorsey, and
Twitter

MARY-LANE KAMBERG

ROSEN PUBLISHING®

New York

For Ronin

Published in 2013 by The Rosen Publishing Group, Inc.
29 East 21st Street, New York, NY 10010

Copyright © 2013 by The Rosen Publishing Group, Inc.

First Edition

All rights reserved. No part of this book may be reproduced in any form without permission in writing from the publisher, except by a reviewer.

Library of Congress Cataloging-in-Publication Data

Kamberg, Mary-Lane, 1948–
Evan Williams, Biz Stone, Jack Dorsey, and Twitter/Mary-Lane Kamberg.—1st ed.
    p. cm.—(Internet biographies)
Includes bibliographical references and index.
ISBN 978-1-4488-6913-8 (library binding)
1. Twitter—Juvenile literature. 2. Microblogs—Juvenile literature.
3. Businessmen—United States—Biography—Juvenile literature.
4. Williams, Evan, 1972—Juvenile literature. 5. Stone, Biz—Juvenile literature.
6. Dorsey, Jack, 1976—Juvenile literature. I. Title.
HM743.T95K36 2013
338.7'610040922—dc23
[B]
                                                                2011048435

Manufactured in the United States of America

CPSIA Compliance Information: Batch #S12YA: For further information, contact Rosen Publishing, New York, New York, at 1-800-237-9932.

Contents

INTRODUCTION

What's happening?

Are you eating a peanut butter and jelly sandwich? Adopting a dog? Meeting your newborn niece? Or, are you watching the Super Bowl? Caught in a hurricane? Taking cover as tanks roll down the street in a developing country?

That's what Twitter users want to know.

Twitter is a social network. It lets you send short messages over cell phones and other devices, as well as the Internet. Some have called it a microblogging service. The messages are like very, very short blogs—no more than 140 characters per post. They fall between blogging and instant messaging.

Twitter is a way to stay connected with friends. It's also an international marketing and communications tool for businesses. And it's becoming an important source of news worldwide. As of March 21, 2011, Twitter had two hundred million users worldwide, according to Cybermedia India Online Limited (CIOL). And it was adding more than 460,000 new accounts per day. Just five years after its release to the public, it was servicing 140 billion messages—called tweets—per day, according to *PC Magazine*.

A casual dress code and innovative interior design contribute to the creative environment at Twitter's offices in San Francisco. The social media's founders share interests in computer technology and the Internet.

Twitter was founded by three creative, inventive college dropouts. Ev Williams, Biz Stone, and Jack Dorsey grew up hundreds of miles apart. But in the 1990s they each developed an interest in computers, as well as something barely known at the time: the Internet. They eventually joined forces in San Francisco. They founded one of the most successful services to keep people in touch.

However, success can be defined in different ways. As Stone said at the 2011 Aspen Ideas Festival, "You should be able to have a positive impact on the world."

Its founders could never have imagined how fast the program would grow.

Even as Twitter added new users in the millions, technical problems followed its extraordinary growth. The service experienced downtime that often irritated users. And its founders had trouble figuring out a way to make money at what they were doing. They all agreed that what they had created was valuable. Unfortunately, no one seemed able to put that value into specific financial terms.

Personal Twitter accounts are free. All you have to do is visit the Twitter Web site. Enter your name, e-mail address, and a password of your choice, and you're ready to tweet! You can also add your photo and a short bio. Next choose friends or celebrities to "follow." If you follow someone, it means you'll receive that person's tweets. You can follow almost anyone registered on the service. Or, you can search by message subject instead of person. In short, according to founder Stone, Twitter is a place for "bursts of activity and randomness."

You can also reply to someone's message, forward it to others (retweet), and use search engines like Google and Yahoo! to find information posted on Twitter. Businesses use Twitter to advertise their wares and update customers on sales or special events. Marketing activities that use tweets seem more personal to consumers than such ordinary mass communications as newspapers, radio, and television.

CHAPTER 1

From Failure to Success: @ev

How did the "black sheep" of a Nebraska farm family become one of the movers and shakers of the Internet social media world?

He started with a lot of failures.

Evan "Ev" Williams became one of the founders of Twitter. But it was a long, hard road to success.

Williams is known in the "Twitterverse" (Twitter universe) as @ev. Born in Clarks, Nebraska, on March 31, 1972, Williams grew up on a farm. Clarks is a small town in south-central Nebraska. It lies about 90 miles (145 kilometers) north and west of Lincoln, the state capital. In 2011, the town's Web site listed the population as 379.

Like all farm kids, Williams helped with daily chores. He irrigated the corn and soybeans. He helped with the cattle. But he often felt out of place. He liked reading books about Babe Ruth or dinosaurs more than hunting with his

Ev Williams was a small-town boy who never felt like he belonged until he moved to Silicon Valley and met others who shared his interest in computers, technology, the Internet—and inventing things.

father and brother. And he thought more about ideas for new inventions than farming.

He once tried to build an oxygen tank so that he could breathe underwater. He used some plastic tubing and a couple of empty soda pop bottles. He also tried to make wings out of plywood so that he could fly.

In school he was part of a class of fourteen. He cared little about his schoolwork. However, like many kids in small towns, he joined in most of the school's extracurricular activities. Again, he felt like he didn't fit in. He was more of a quiet loner than a joiner. Still, he played sports, and he played in the band.

For his senior year he moved to Columbus, Nebraska. Columbus's population is about twenty thousand, according to the city's Web site. It lies about 80 miles (129 km) west of Omaha. Although the population is higher than Clarks,

After high school, Ev Williams enrolled at the Lincoln campus at the University of Nebraska. He stayed only three semesters before striking out to join the workforce in Florida and Texas.

Columbus is still a small town. It was founded as a railroad hub. Later it became famous as the place where Buffalo Bill held the first full dress rehearsal of his Wild West Show. Williams graduated from Columbus High School in 1990. (Twenty years later on the school's alumni Web site, he listed his interests as the Internet, dining, design, blogs, clocks, vegetarians, and blogging.)

WASTING TIME?

After high school, Williams went to the University of Nebraska at Lincoln. He joined the FarmHouse International Fraternity. The fraternity is an agricultural social group founded at the Missouri College of Agriculture in 1905. Williams took just a few classes. He lacked focus. And he never cared enough about any subject area to declare a major.

Williams was eager to join the workforce. And the longer he stayed in college, the more he thought he was wasting time. He had lots of ideas for new businesses, and he was drawn to computers and the Internet. After only a year and a half, he dropped out of college.

With little sense of purpose, he moved to Florida. In Key West, he found work as a freelance copywriter. Copywriting may include such assignments as advertising, newsletters, pubic relations, or other types of writing.

Williams also worked at several information technology (IT) jobs at start-up companies in Key West. IT is the branch of engineering that deals with computer hardware and software. Work in IT creates, organizes, stores, and communicates data. A start-up company is a new business still in the research and development stage.

For Williams, nothing really caught on. He moved to Texas and found more IT work in Dallas and Austin. He lived with his older sister for a while. He spent time coming up with ideas for new businesses. But none of them developed into working companies. In 1993, with nothing going for him and little ambition, he moved back home.

A FAMILY BUSINESS

In Nebraska, Williams and his father started his first company in 1994. It was based in Lincoln. The company produced CD-ROMs and a video about how to use the Internet. A CD-ROM is a compact disk used with a computer instead of a traditional music player. It acts as read-only memory. A user cannot change the information on it. The Williamses' biggest hit was a CD-ROM for University of Nebraska football fans.

In 1995 people outside the military were first learning about the Internet. Almost overnight eighteen million people began using the Internet for commercial purposes, according to Andrew Beattie at Investopedia.com. The father-son team knew little about the World Wide Web. But Williams could see its future. Still, neither could write software, and there was little money to grow the business.

At one point, Williams learned to design Web sites. His company hosted some sites for other people. But soon he grew bored of developing other people's projects. The work didn't satisfy his desire to build a business and be his own boss. He also felt a bit disorganized, starting projects and abandoning them in favor of newer ideas.

While Williams was making his way in Nebraska, the real action in the high-tech world was in California. The region, nicknamed Silicon Valley, includes the Santa Clara Valley, the San Jose metropolitan area, the southern San Francisco peninsula, and the southern section of the East Bay. The nickname originated in 1971. It first referred to the region's large number of silicon chip inventors and manufacturers. A silicon chip is an important piece of high-tech hardware. Today, the term "Silicon Valley" refers to all types of high-tech companies in the area.

Williams learned all he could about the Silicon Valley start-ups. He tried to mimic their activities. The problem was that he had little business experience. He'd never held a "real" job at an established company. And, of course, he'd never run one. He lacked the skills students learn in business schools at colleges and universities.

Williams couldn't manage people. Some employees became angry and resentful. Williams also had trouble with finances. He couldn't keep track of the money. He failed to pay payroll taxes and owed money to the Internal Revenue Service (IRS)—not a situation a young man (or an older one, either) wants to be in. Over five years, three of his ventures failed. He lost money on all of them. He also lost the stake his father put up to start them. He was forced to close the companies. (After some later business success, Ev Williams paid back his father.)

A LEAP OF FAITH

By 1997, Williams had little money and no job possibilities. The future looked bleak. So he took a chance and headed for Silicon Valley. His first home in California was in a small farming town called Sebastopol, about 50 miles (80 km) north of San Francisco. Sebastopol echoed his farming roots, so he must have felt comfortable in his new home.

He got his first job in the marketing department of O'Reilly Inc., a media/conference company now called O'Reilly Media. He finally found out what it was like to work in an office; it wasn't for him. During his seven months with O'Reilly, Williams learned the technical skills he needed to work in Web development. He quit as an O'Reilly employee, becoming a freelancer for the company writing computer code. He later took on additional freelance Web development clients, including Intel Corporation and Hewlett-Packard Company.

BUILDING A COMPANY

As the millennium approached, Williams and his girlfriend, Meg Hourihan, teamed up to found Pyra Labs. The company created computer software for project management. The programs made it easier for managers to coordinate projects online.

About the same time, Williams and Hourihan began writing Weblogs. A Weblog is an Internet site—or part of a site—where individuals post regular entries. Examples include online diaries, vacation activities, business-related topics, or opinion pieces. Williams and Hourihan found blogging hard to manage. So they wrote a program to make the process easier. The two used it to take and share notes on their projects. The system became the prototype for a new program.

Some credit Williams with coming up with the word "blog," which is short for "Weblog." At least, he made the term popular. He called the new program Blogger. Williams decided to turn Blogger into its own company as a blog publishing service. Before Blogger was formed, only the most experienced techies wrote blogs. And those were directed at a few specialized readers. Most blogs contained

Ev Williams and his then girlfriend, Meg Hourihan, founded a start-up company called Pyra Labs. They developed a new software program called Blogger that made writing blogs easy and more accessible.

only opinion pieces or links to other Internet sites. Blogger adapted the idea for the general public. It was one of the first companies to give users a way to create their own on-line journals. Those users became known as bloggers.

THE DOT-COM BUBBLE

In early 2000, Williams found himself in the right place at what seemed to be the right time. Since about 1995, interest in the Internet caught the attention of investors. The new

users meant a new market. Speculators put money in high-tech companies. Lots of it.

At first, investors cared more about big ideas than big profits. They counted on new technology to produce big profits in the future. So they risked money in the hopes of making a profit once the businesses caught on. On paper, the stocks for some public companies appeared to be gaining value. But the risk was high. Soon after many companies' stocks went up for sale, they reported huge losses. Others simply went out of business.

The National Association of Securities Dealers Automated Quotations (NASDAQ) is an American electronic stock market for high-tech stocks. The NASDAQ 100 includes the largest domestic and international technology companies. Its composite value reached a peak of 5046.86 on March 11, 2000. The period of time between 1995 and 2000 has been called the dot-com bubble.

RAISING SEED MONEY

Blogger was not a public company listed on the NASDAQ. Instead, Williams raised seed money directly from investors. Seed money is money invested in start-up firms and small businesses seeking to expand. It is also known

@EV's Recognition and Awards

During his career, several magazines have honored and recognized Ev Williams for his work on Twitter. He was included on the following lists:

2007 "50 Who Matter Now," *Business 2.0*

2009 "The World's Most Influential People," *TIME*

2009 "100 Agents of Change," *Rolling Stone*

2009 "40 under 40," *Fortune*

2010 "40 under 40," *Fortune*

as venture capital. Investors get part ownership in the company—and a say in the decision-making process. Such investors, known as venture capitalists, expect higher returns than they could get with other investment choices.

Williams used the seed money to hire employees at Blogger. Soon after Williams secured his financing, the dot-com bubble burst. On October 9, 2001, the NASDAQ composite lost 78 percent of its value. It dropped to

1114.11. With such a loss among technology stocks, investors in new technology start-up companies became scarce.

Alas, Williams still didn't know how to make money. While some revenues flowed in, they weren't enough to keep Blogger in business. And because the high-tech market had crashed, there was little—if any—money available from investors. Williams had to lay off all of his employees. His cofounder, Meg Hourihan, refused to be laid off. She quit instead. With no employees, Williams ran the company by himself from his home for two years. Then he started a premium version of Blogger that increased income for the company.

Williams later told Inc.com that the business accomplishment he was most proud of was "not letting Blogger die." He didn't know it yet. But he was one step closer to becoming a Twitter founder.

Williams now lives in the San Francisco Bay area with his wife, Sara Morishige Williams, a designer from San Jose, California. They have a son named Miles. Despite growing up on a cattle farm, Williams is now a vegetarian. He may be shy, but he's not snobbish. It's just that he prefers to stay out of the spotlight. In October 2010, Sarah Lacy, senior editor of TechCrunch.com, called him "the nice guy in Silicon Valley."

CHAPTER 2

From Artist to Entrepreneur: @biz

With his somewhat goofy look, rumpled hairstyle, and black-rimmed glasses, Christopher Isaac "Biz" Stone became the second founder of Twitter. He also became known as the "face" of the company. Unlike Williams, who hangs back in crowds, Stone is outgoing and easy to talk to. He thrives in the limelight. He became Twitter's main spokesman on television and in interviews for other media.

Stone was born on March 10, 1974, in Boston. He grew up in the Boston suburb of Wellesley, Massachusetts, a college town about 18 miles (29 km) southwest of the city. Wellesley is home to three colleges: Wellesley College, Babson College, and Massachusetts Bay Community College.

As a toddler Stone mispronounced Christopher as "Biz-ah-bah." His mother started calling him "Biz." His father was also named Christopher. The nickname made it easier to not confuse father and son in conversations. At

As an adult, Biz Stone's interest in computers overtook his early interest in art, literature, and drama. Still, his early experience in theater paid off when he later became the face of Twitter in the media.

Biz Stone's third-grade birthday party, his friends heard his mother call him "Biz." His classmates picked it up, and it stuck. From then on, except for his official "Isaac Stone" name for business documents and checks, he's been known as Biz. On Twitter he's @biz.

Stone attended Wellesley High School, where he dreamed of becoming a businessman. Stone tried out for the school's sports teams, and coaches cut him from all of them. Even then, as now, he had no fear of failure. He learned to negotiate. (He would use those skills later in the business world.) He still wanted to play a high school sport and noticed that his school had no lacrosse team. He went to the school administration and proposed starting one. The administration approved. No one knew much about the sport, but the team was pretty good. And it turned out Stone turned was good at it, too. The team elected him captain.

Stone started out as an artist—and at times the class clown. He discovered an early love for graphic arts, literature, theater, and design. When he was a senior, school officials canceled the senior play. Again, Stone stepped up and coordinated the event himself. He starred in a humorous version of *Robin Hood*.

The record is unclear whether the comedy was intentional or resulted from Stone's lack of acting ability. The fact remains that as an adult he was at ease in front of television cameras and in the show business environment.

OFF TO COLLEGE

Stone graduated from Wellesley High School in 1992. As a boy, he wanted to earn a degree from Babson College. The school is known for its focus on business leadership.

Instead, when the time came, he got a scholarship to Northeastern University, a private research university in Boston. He majored in English but left after the first year.

The next year, he transferred to the University of Massachusetts Boston, a public research university. He studied humanities on a theater arts scholarship. At best, Stone was a preoccupied student. In 1994, while still at UMass Boston, he took a job at Little, Brown and Company, a publisher on Beacon Hill. Beacon Hill is an affluent neighborhood in Boston known for its famous former residents, including poet Robert Frost, author Louisa Mae Alcott, Edwin Thomas Booth (brother of Abraham Lincoln's assassin, John Wilkes Booth), and others.

Stone's job at Little, Brown was moving boxes. But he knew about graphic design, and he was at home on a Macintosh computer. Little, Brown's graphic arts department had just switched to Macs. The art department was working on a book jacket design.

One day Stone found himself alone in the office. Everyone else had gone to lunch. He plopped down in front of one of the computers. He designed a book jacket of his own. He slipped it into the stack of covers designed by the graphic

Biz Stone studied theater arts at the University of Massachusetts Boston campus. But his part-time job in publishing held more interest than his classes. He dropped out of school and went to work there full-time.

designers. A week later, the client chose Stone's creation. The art director came looking for the person who made it.

Stone later told *GQ*, "When I said, 'It was me,' the art director asked, "What, the box guy?"

He promoted Stone to book designer.

VENTURING OUT

Stone had achieved his dream of becoming a businessman. He dropped out of college.

He stayed at Little, Brown for three years. He later told *GQ* what he learned during that time. "There is not just one great design for a book cover," he said.

Years later Stone spoke at the commencement ceremony at Babson College—the school he once dreamed of attending. He told graduates, "I learned the value of creativity when I dropped out of college. Creativity is a renewable resource. Be as creative as you like, as often as you like, because you can never run out."

Web design and programming came naturally to Stone. So in the late 1990s, when a friend suggested an idea for a social networking and blogging community, Stone came aboard and took the title of creative trainer. In 2000, founders Marc Ginsburg, John Hiller, and Dan Huddle launched Xanga to the public.

Today, Xanga is a free service. Users create audio, photo, and video blogs. They also use the service for social networking. Xanga is popular with teenagers. It is also a big hit in Asia. In addition to English, Xanga supports users in such languages as Chinese, Spanish, Indonesian, Japanese, and Korean.

A year after joining Xanga, Stone felt discontent. He decided to leave and moved to Los Angeles. In Los Angeles, Stone worked in television for a while, and he wrote his first book; *Blogging: Genius Strategies for Instant Web Content* was published by New Riders Press on September 21, 2002. After that, Stone returned to Boston. He worked at the Wellesley College Alumni Association.

HELPING OTHERS

If Williams was Twitter's money man, Stone was its social conscience. He wanted to "do more good in the world."

In the commencement speech at Babson College, he told students, "People too often consider altruism only after they have achieved financial success. This approach is flawed because it does not take into account the value of helping others."

Stone believes that "when we help others, we also help ourselves." He would like to see a new way of doing business—with higher goals and a better, more selfless way to measure success. He thinks value should be more important than profit. And he thinks that helping others gives deep meaning to his work.

In 2008, Stone won a debate about whether entrepreneurs can influence positive change that relates to global challenges. The debate was held at the Oxford Union, a debate society in Oxford, England. Most of its members come from Oxford University, where Stone annually teaches a master class at the Saïd Business School. Stone also teaches classes at the Haas School of Business at the University of California, Berkeley.

While the other Twitter founders keep their private lives private, Stone readily shares some of his away-from-work favorites. He drives a Mini Cooper. His most used gadgets are the iPhone and MacBook Air. However, because he works with computer hardware all day, he keeps high-tech devices hidden out of sight at home. He likes Sherlock Holmes mysteries. On television, his favorite shows include *House*, *The Vampire Diaries*, *Entourage*, and *True Blood*. His favorite meal is vegan pizza delivered from Amici's East Coast Pizzeria.

COMPASSION FOR ANIMALS

In keeping with his "helping others" philosophy, Stone founded or became involved in several organizations. Among them is the nonprofit Biz and Livia Stone Foundation, which he and his wife founded. The group supports education and conservation in California. It also supports other organizations with similar goals. Its programs include arts education grants, after-school activities, and on-site field trips.

The arts grants program pays for supplies for art projects at schools that can't pay for them. The after-school program has included such activities as camping, soccer, swimming, and Hawaiian jujitsu. On-site field trips bring conservation programs to the classroom. One is a program by the Marine Mammal Center, a rescue and rehabilitation center for sick and injured marine mammals. The other is presented by WildCare Bay Area, a wildlife hospital and education center.

Stone acts on the couple's compassion for animals. For one thing, Biz Stone is a vegan. A vegan is a strict vegetarian who eats no fish, meat, chicken, eggs, or milk. The couple has adopted rescue dogs and cats, and even a tortoise. And they advocate pet adoption, rather than buying an animal from a pet store.

But that's only the beginning. Livia Stone once worked at WildCare and still volunteers there. It's not unusual for her husband to come home and find sick or injured bats, owls, gophers, or skunks temporarily sharing his home. The couple also supports Farm Sanctuary, a national farm animal protection organization.

Arianna Huffington (*second from left*) honored "2010 Game Changers" Cory Booker (*left*), mayor of Newark, New Jersey, as well as Livia and Biz Stone. Huffington recognized the Stones for their public service and philanthropy.

In 2010, the Huffington Post honored Biz and Livia Stone, mentioning their public service and "amazing philanthropy work."

WORKING FOR SOCIAL CHANGE

In 2011, Biz Stone was founding director and cochair of ConvergeUS, a nonprofit organization based in Washington, D.C. His cofounder was Rey Ramsey, chief executive officer of TechNet.org, which is a bipartisan, political network of chief executive officers (CEOs) and senior executives of technology companies. Companies represented include Twitter, Cisco, Deloitte Strategic Services, Comcast, and Kaboom!

ConvergeUS joins forces with other nonprofit organizations or academic institutions. They annually select up to three projects. Each project uses technology to work on such social issues as early childhood education, the environment, and the needs of American military families.

Shortly after cofounding ConvergeUS, Stone also signed on as a strategic adviser for social impact at AOL. AOL is the American global Internet services media company once called America Online. Stone helps the leadership team there develop AOL's philanthropic strategies. He also advises at least seven other charities and organizations.

AWARDS AND RECOGNITION

Stone belongs to the International Academy of Digital Arts & Sciences, a professional organization for Internet technology and achievement. When he talks about his career, he stresses the importance of creativity, learning from mistakes, and "celebrating the triumph of humanity through technology."

Top Twitter Abbreviations

If you try to tweet with too many characters, you'll get a message asking you to "be more creative." To cut the text to the allowed number, use one or more of these Twitter abbreviations:

b/c = because

b4 = before

bfn = bye for now

btw =by the way

da = the

deets = details

em = email

fav = favorite

fb = facebook

ftf = face-to-face

gr8 = great

ic = I see

jk = just kidding

k = okay

L8 = late

L8er = later

lmk = let me know

lol = laugh out loud

oh = overheard

peeps = people

plz = please

ppl = people

ru? = are you?

r = are

thx or tx = thanks

ttyl = talk to you later

ttys = talk to you soon

tyt = take your time

ty = thank you

u = you

ur = your

v2v = voice to voice (by phone)

yw = you're welcome

He tells interviewers, "In order to succeed spectac-ularly, you must be ready to fail spectacularly." He also believes that people can make their own opportunities. Instead of waiting around for the right set of circum-stances, "you can create those sets of circumstances on your own."

In 2004, *PC Magazine* named Stone one of its "People of the Year" for his work on Blogger. Five years later, *GQ* named him "2009 Nerd of the Year." The same year Inc. com called him the "Entrepreneur of the Decade," and *TIME* magazine named him one of the "World's Most In-fluential People." He made *Fortune* magazine's lists of "40 Under 40" in both 2009 and 2010. And *Vanity Fair* chose him among the "Top Ten Most Influential People of the Information Age."

Among other honors and awards, Stone has earned the Innovation Award from the International Center for Journalism. And in 2011 Babson College awarded him an honorary doctor of laws degree.

Chapter 3

Ideas R Us: @jack

Today, Jack Dorsey is a soft-spoken adult. Friends describe him as calm and cool, but intense. In elementary school he was a quiet youngster with an idea. At the age of eight, he first got inklings of an idea for the service that would become Twitter. By fourteen, he had developed the first version of the software.

Dorsey, who is known as @jack, was born in St. Louis, Missouri, on November 19, 1976. As a boy, he loved things that move. He loved trains; he and his brother used to go down to the tracks to watch them roll by. But Jack Dorsey loved cars, trucks, bicycles, ambulances, and fire trucks more. He loved the bustle of the city as vehicles made their way through streets and intersections. He became curious about how cities work.

This interest translated into an interest in city maps. Dorsey became so fascinated with them, he taught himself how to write computer code so that he could make his

Jack Dorsey taught himself to write computer software. He got his first job as a programmer at the age of fifteen. His boss, Jim McKelvey, put him in charge of other programmers who were adults.

own. His maps showed not only where the streets were, but also movement along them. He used the maps to design ways to route taxis, messengers, delivery trucks, and emergency vehicles through busy city streets.

He found that he had a talent for programming. He offered his program as open source software. Open source software is a free program that includes the program's source code. A source code is text written in a computer programming language. People can use open source software "as is" or customize it to their own uses. The code Dorsey wrote at the age of fourteen was still used to send taxis to riders in 2011.

HIGH SCHOOL DAYS

Dorsey attended Bishop DuBourg High School, a private Roman Catholic high school in St. Louis, Missouri. Classmates describe him as not particularly popular. But they remember his enthusiasm for the Internet—something most of them knew little about.

But some companies in the area were well aware of it. Mira Digital Publishing was one of them. One of its employees was a customer at the coffee shop Dorsey's mother,

Marcia, owned. Over a cup of coffee, the customer mentioned that his company was desperately looking for programmers.

Marcia Dorsey introduced him to her fifteen-year-old son. The company hired Jack Dorsey as a summer intern. After running errands and doing simple computer tasks, Dorsey told company owner Jack McKelvey that he should be doing business on the Internet. McKelvey agreed. He hired additional programmers and told them to do whatever Dorsey said. They did, and Dorsey discovered that he could manage people.

Dorsey continued to work on his mapping software. He and his brother even started their own company. It was a bicycle courier service that used the program Jack Dorsey wrote. Unfortunately, the business failed for lack of customers.

HEADING TO COLLEGE— AND BEYOND

Dorsey graduated from high school in 1995. He headed for the University of Missouri at Rolla (later renamed the Missouri University of Science and Technology). The school was known as the place to go for engineering students interested in computer technology, including creating computer games. And it was close to home, just 109 miles (175 km) southwest of St. Louis.

Jim McKelvey, who took a chance and hired fifteen-year-old Jack Dorsey, later partnered with him to found a new electronic payment service called Square. The device lets businesses and individuals swipe payment cards on a mobile device.

Along with his college studies, Dorsey stayed interested in cities and his dispatch programs for them. He researched companies that used a dispatch method to send messengers, delivery trucks, and emergency vehicles on their way. During his sophomore year, he stumbled upon the Web site of Dispatch Management Services Corporation (DMSC). The business managed dispatch centers for couriers—on foot, bicycles, and motorcycles—in major cities in the United States, as well as the United Kingdom, New Zealand, and Australia. The corporation, which was based in Delaware, had offices in New York City.

For Dorsey it must have seemed like a call from his future. What better place than the Big Apple to try out his ideas? Dorsey spent a lot of time navigating the Web site. He also got into sections intended to be locked out against nonemployees. He learned that Greg Kidd was the company founder, as well as the chairman of the board of directors. And he found Kidd's e-mail address.

Dorsey sent Kidd a message. He described how he gained access to the employee-only sections of the corporate Web site. He also told Kidd how to repair the security breakdown. Dorsey later told author Jeffrey Bussman what else he said to Kidd. "I said, 'I'm writing some dispatch software, and I'd really love to come to New York and work with you all.'"

Dorsey soon heard back from Kidd, who hired him for the Manhattan office in New York. Dorsey took the job and transferred to New York University. He was finally writing code for a dispatch company. And learning a lot.

HEADING WEST

After a while, Kidd and Dorsey wanted to improve dispatch software. But they wanted to start a new company to do it. Kidd resigned as chairman and director of DMSC in November 1998. With only one semester to go for a bachelor's degree from NYU, Dorsey dropped out of school. He recognized the opportunity to realize his lifelong dreams in California. And he knew he could finish his degree later.

The two moved to Oakland, California. They got seed money from a group of Silicon Valley executives who invest in start-up technology companies. Kidd and Dorsey named the new company dNET, for Dispatch Network. The idea was to provide a Web-based dispatch system that also let couriers get paid via the Internet. The founders hired an outside chief executive officer so that they could do the programming.

The idea for dNET's product seemed like a good one. But finding a customer base dragged on. The company wasn't making enough money. When the

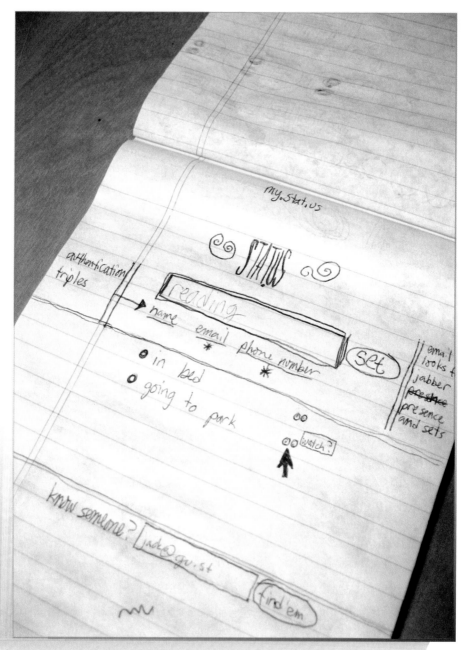

One night in 2000, Jack Dorsey got out of bed and jotted down notes for a program that could gather, send, and save e-mails in real time. Dorsey called his program Stat.us, a forerunner of Twitter.

dot-com bubble burst, companies like dNET were on shaky ground. Kidd and Dorsey argued with the company's CEO about what to do. The CEO had his way. He laid off both founders.

THE FIRST HINT OF TWITTER

While Dorsey was working with dNET, he also became aware of a new set of technologies called instant messaging (IM). The text-based, real-time communication connected two or more users over the Internet. IM is a form of online chat. For real-time messages, users had to be at their computer keyboards at the same time. Dorsey liked the idea of being able to see what his friends were listening to, what they were working on, and what they were doing.

At the time Dorsey owned a small e-mail device called the RIM 850. It was the predecessor to the BlackBerry. One night in 2000, he couldn't sleep. He got up and wrote a simple program he could use to collect incoming e-mails, send them out, and record them so that he could read them on the Internet. This script was another stepping stone in the evolution of Twitter. Dorsey called it Stat.us.

Of course, he wanted to try it out. So he entered five friends' e-mail addresses into the program. He went for a walk and took his RIM 850 along. He ended up at the Golden Gate Park Buffalo Paddock, a bison grazing area in San Francisco's Golden Gate Park. He sent a group e-mail to his five friends: "I'm at the Bison Paddock watching the bison."

The First @whitehouse Twitter Town Hall: #AskObama

Twitter has added a new take on the traditional political town hall. In a usual town hall meeting, a politician meets with voters in his or her home district. At the meetings, elected officials—or candidates running for office—stand on stage, in person. Citizens line up to ask questions about current issues.

On July 6, 2011, Twitter founder Jack Dorsey hosted the first Twitter national town hall with President Barack Obama. The event, which had a live audience, was webcast from the East Room of the White House. White House staff also tweeted the meeting through the @whitehouse feed.

More than 110,000 tweets used the #@AskObama hashtag to ask questions about jobs, the economy, the budget, taxes, and education. Dots on a map of the United States showed viewers the location of each tweet as it was asked and answered.

On July 6, 2011, Twitter made history with the first Twitter town hall meeting in the East Room of the White House. With Twitter founder Jack Dorsey on hand, President Barack Obama fielded questions from 110,000 tweets.

It was meant as an instant message. But the e-mails simply sat in the friends' in-boxes. The communication was read only when the friends checked their e-mails. That took the "instant" out of the process. Dorsey also realized that his friends weren't likely to be interested in what he was doing anyway. But the idea wouldn't leave Dorsey alone. He continued to tweak the program, hoping someday its time would come.

MOVING HOME

When Dorsey found himself unemployed from dNET, he knew another computer job would be hard to find. Even if he found an opening, he'd have to compete with hundreds of other programmers laid off from other technology companies. Dorsey moved home to St. Louis and went to work for his father.

During his time in St. Louis, Jack Dorsey toyed with the idea of pursuing different careers. He was a good artist. He could illustrate flowers. His thought process took another turn when he injured his wrist. His treatment included massage therapy. Dorsey became interested in the field. He took the required training course and became a certified massage therapist. But he kept wanting to return to California. Finally, he followed his heart and moved to San Francisco.

He found that jobs as a massage therapist were as hard to find as programming ones. So he took some odd jobs, even babysitting his former dNET partner Kidd's daughter. Dorsey also found some freelance work as a programmer. One of his projects was writing software used for printing tickets for tours of Alcatraz Island, a former prison known as "the Rock."

Dorsey has a wide variety of interests. In fact, he's somewhat of a "fashionista." He describes his own clothing style as "rustic elegant." But he is inspired by fashion designers' creativity. He has followed the world of fashion for years. In 2009, he surprised participants when he attended the annual Council of Fashion Designers of America (CFDA) Awards. He was pleased to have been invited by then CFDA president Diane von Fürstenberg.

A few years earlier, along with his work at Odeo and then Obvious, Dorsey became interested in making his own jeans. He took classes in fashion design and sewing. Along with the other students, he started with skirts. It was a good choice because they're easier to make than pants. Dorsey worked with such styles as pencil and asymmetrical skirts. Unfortunately for Dorsey's fashion career, Twitter took off. He had to quit before they got to pants.

AN UNLIKELY ENTREPRENEUR

Dorsey didn't think of himself as an entrepreneur. And in the early days of his career, he didn't look like one either. He wore ear and nose rings. He wore his hair either in dreadlocks or in what can only be described as a moplike style. He also has a tattoo in the shape of a collarbone that runs the length of his forearm.

Dorsey's attitude toward his work doesn't sound like an entrepreneur either. He places more importance on the process of creating something than any profit he might make from it. And he cares little or nothing for the material things success can bring. He rarely drives a car; he prefers walking. And he lives in a one-bedroom apartment just one block from his office.

Still, Dorsey's work has led him to create several businesses along the way. In an interview with CelebrityNetWorth.com, he said, "When you have a clear vision of what you want to do in the world, everything works out. When you're driving toward that passion and love, you can figure out the mechanics. You can create a business around it."

Dorsey has earned recognition for his work. In 2008, he was named by the Massachusetts Institute of Technology's *Technology Review* as one of the top thirty-five innovators in the world under the age of thirty-five. In 2009, *TIME* magazine called him one of "the World's Most Influential People." *Business Week* magazine acknowledged him as one of "Technology's Best & Brightest Young Entrepreneurs." In 2009, Dorsey served as a member of the advisory board of Ustream.tv, a Web site that provides a platform for live video streaming of events online.

CHAPTER 4

Coming Together

In early 2003, the first two Twitter founders joined forces. After "meeting" Biz Stone via blogging and e-mail, Ev Williams invited him to work at Blogger. But in February, after four months of negotiations, Williams sold Pyra Labs to the Internet search engine company Google. The amount was undisclosed, but Williams later used some of the money to start the company that gave birth to Twitter.

At the time of the sale, Blogger served one million blogs. But, according to the *Guardian* newspaper, only two hundred thousand of them were active. As part of the deal, Williams joined Google as an employee. Stone joined Williams just as Google bought Blogger. By Google's standards neither was "qualified" to work there. Neither had a degree, but Google hired them both as part of the deal.

As Stone later told *GQ* magazine, Williams had e-mailed and asked him to come to work at Blogger. Stone accepted the job and headed west. However, he said, "There was no way Google would have hired me, because I didn't finish college." Williams went to bat for Stone, and Google hired him, too. Stone signed on as a senior specialist. At Google, Stone helped grow Blogger globally.

The two stayed at Google for twenty months. They both say they "thoroughly enjoyed" it. At Google, Williams met designer Sara Emilia Morishige, who also worked there. (They married in 2007.) While Stone was at Google, he published his second book. St. Martin's Griffin Publishing released *Who Let the Blogs Out? A Hyperconnected Peek at the World of Weblogs* in 2004.

In October 2004, Stone and Williams left Google to strike out on their own. As Stone later told the *Wall Street Journal*, "It was about the toughest decision I ever made, and if I'd known how high Google stock would go, I'm not sure I would have made it."

When Williams left Google, he had enough money "not to work," but he was still interested in creating new businesses.

THE FORGOTTEN FOUNDER: @NOAH

Williams's next business was a podcasting company. Another entrepreneur named Noah Glass lived next door to Williams. The two had opposite personalities. Compared to Williams's deliberate, quiet manner, Glass was impulsive and, at times, explosive. Although Glass has been largely ignored as a Twitter founder, he played an important role in its development. Some have called him "the forgotten founder." His Twitter bio says simply, "i started this."

Williams secured some venture capital. He and Glass founded Odeo, Inc. They located their office in the South Park neighborhood of San Francisco, an area around South Park Street and Second Street that some have called the best-kept secret in the city. Williams and Glass wanted to build a central directory for audio on the Internet. Users could use it to search, download, and listen to any audio on the World Wide Web. They could also design their own podcasts. Stone joined Odeo in 2005 as director of community.

Glass and Williams together developed Audioblogger. It was a service that let users leave audio messages on their blogs. The messages became audio blog posts. (The service ceased operation on November 1, 2006.)

@JACK COMES ABOARD

While Williams, Glass, and Stone were busy at Odeo, Dorsey had moved back to California. He was working odd jobs and doing freelance programming—and looking for a permanent, full-time job.

Soon after Williams (*left*) resigned from Google, he met Noah Glass (*right*). The two developed Audioblogger, a service that let users leave audio messages on their blogs. Glass later became known as Twitter's "forgotten founder."

Dorsey had followed Williams's blog for some time. Dorsey knew about Williams's career accomplishments and the latest venture with Odeo. Dorsey wanted to work with him. He had heard that Odeo needed a programmer. One day in 2005, Dorsey saw Williams on the street. He introduced himself and asked Williams for a job. Williams hired Dorsey on a trial basis, and Dorsey went to work on a program to download Webcasts from the Internet to users' computers, iPods, or MP3 players. While working on this task, Dorsey and Glass became close friends.

During this time a co-worker at Odeo showed Dorsey a text message service that she used a lot. Short message service (SMS) lets users communicate short messages over the Internet, phones, or

What's Twitter Worth?

Everything—a car, a World Series championship ring, or a business—is worth whatever someone is willing to pay for it and a seller is willing to accept. With that in mind, no one really knows Twitter's value. And since the founders say they don't want to sell the company, it could be said to be priceless.

Here are some estimates reported in various media at various times.

2009: $500 million to $1 billion

Early in the year, EncompassSocial. com reported that Twitter turned down a $500 million offer from Facebook. Some estimates of Twitter's value reached $1 billion.

2010: $3.7 billion to $4 billion

In December 2010, *TheBlaze.com* estimated Twitter's value at $3.7 billion after the company raised $200 million in funding. In February 2011, Twitter's value jumped to $4 billion after the company raised another $80 million.

2011: $8 billion to $10 billion

In February 2011, *New Media Age* reported that Twitter was in talks with both Facebook and Google. Estimates of Twitter's value rose again.

2011: $4.5 billion

In March, Biz Stone denied rumors that Twitter would sell a 10 percent share to JPMorgan Chase & Company for $450 million, suggesting Twitter's total value at ten times that.

July 2011: $7 billion

Twitter announced it would seek another round of financing. *TheBlaze.com* upped the company's value to $7 billion.

mobile communication devices. It had been around since the 1980s, but Dorsey knew little about it. He loved it, and he wondered, what if users could set their status and archive it on the Internet using SMS—and it all happened in real time? Dorsey's idea materialized just in time.

Apple Inc. introduced iTunes on January 9, 2001. At first, iTunes focused only on recorded music. But by June 2005—as Odeo's engineers worked on its podcasting software—Apple added podcasts to its product. Apple would be a fierce competitor. Worse, Apple's new program made much of the work Odeo was doing unnecessary, if not obsolete.

Odeo's leadership had to do something. Fast.

Stone asked Williams, "Do you really want to be the King of Podcasting?"

Williams said, "No."

That's all it took for them to look for a way to reinvent the company.

REBOOTING THE COMPANY

Williams divided employees into teams to brainstorm new ideas. Dorsey's group gathered at the South Park neighborhood playground. They were eating Mexican food. Dorsey sat on top of the slide.

He explained his idea for a status update service. A user could use it to tell friends what he or she was doing. For instance, Dorsey said, he might use it to send a short text message to tell friends that the club he was patronizing was "happening." The group understood the idea, and they liked it.

From Dorsey's early attempts to communicate with taxis, messengers, and emergency vehicles to his abandoned experiment at the buffalo park, the time for his idea had finally come. As Dorsey later said, "Some things are worth the wait."

After the all-day brainstorming sessions, the groups returned to Odeo's office. Each discussed its ideas. Dorsey's idea was selected to be developed as a side project. The rest of the employees continued with podcasting work in case Dorsey's idea didn't work out. Dorsey was sure it would. He spent some extra time discussing the idea with Glass and Williams until they, too, were excited about it.

THE BIRD'S THE WORD

Glass managed the team assigned to build a prototype. The team was small. Stone designed the Web site. Dorsey programmed along with Florian Webber, a contractor working off-site from Germany.

The team worked together in a true group effort. Dorsey insisted that they keep the prototype simple. He didn't want users to have to think about what they were doing. He wanted them to be able just to "type something and send it." Glass insisted they keep their work secret. The team spent just two weeks creating the first program for a Web site where users could post short messages.

The project needed a name. Someone suggested Twitch, but it didn't seem quite right. Team members worried that it could easily be abbreviated as "Twit." Glass paged through the *Oxford English Dictionary*, starting

Twitter users can communicate via mobile devices, as well as the Internet. Quick, real-time mobile communication was Twitter founder Jack Dorsey's goal when he first developed software for courier services.

with words that started with "tw." The word "twitter" was defined as chirps of birds or bursts of trivial information. Dorsey said the name described exactly what they were doing. The rest of the team agreed.

They dropped the vowels so that the name had only five letters. That corresponded to the five numbers of text messaging short codes that cell phone companies used for texting. A short code is like a telephone number that users send messages to.

The short code for Twttr would have been 89887. However, the team learned that someone else already owned that number. They changed the name back to Twitter. In keeping with the bird theme, they called the short messages "tweets." Messages were limited to 140 characters. That allowed another fifteen for the user's special Twitter username. The number of characters was based on the SMS limit of 160 characters per message.

LAUNCHING TWITTER

On March 21, 2006, the team launched Twitter. Dorsey sent the first tweet at 12:50 PM: "just setting up my twttr."

Odeo employees started using the service. By July, Twitter was released to the public. Employees became goodwill ambassadors for the status update service. Dom Sagolla, an Odeo employee, later said, "Each one of the original users became a kind of personal evangelist for Twttr, trying to get our coworkers and friends to use it."

Perhaps no one—maybe not even Dorsey—liked the idea as much as Glass. He became Twitter's head cheerleader. He kept raving about the potential success of the service.

Glass lobbied hard to keep Twitter separate from the distraction of the other activities at Odeo. The focus for those activities seemed to alternate between trying to improve Odeo and trying to sell it. Glass wanted to spin off Twitter as its own company. He also wanted to be CEO.

CONFLICTS AND LAYOFFS

The relationship between Odeo's leaders and its board of directors was going south. The podcasting product was becoming useless. And although Twitter held promise, its value was difficult to explain or demonstrate. The board saw Twitter as a distraction from its core business.

They recommended drastic cuts. And in May 2006, four employees were laid off. (These former employees kept using Twitter to stay in touch. And they got their friends to use it.) That summer, in a surprise move, Williams also fired Glass.

Although Williams kept his reasons to himself, others guessed at them. Some said the two had a personality conflict. Others said it was because Glass wanted to spin off Twitter and become CEO. In the end, Williams was the one with the money. He called the shots.

Glass, who had managed the prototype team and was the leading advocate of the Twitter project felt betrayed. He suspended his Twitter account and moved to Los Angeles, where he worked on a gaming program. He also worked on an alternative energy project. He even built a prototype. Unfortunately, it didn't work the way he expected, and the project didn't pan out.

In September, Williams sent a letter to his investors. At the time, Twitter had only five thousand registered users, according to the letter. Williams bought out the Odeo investors with money he got from selling Blogger. Although the exact figure he spent has not been reported, Inc.com says it cost him $3 million, plus "all the money Odeo had." Glass was among the investors Williams paid off.

Williams learned from Odeo's failure. He had raised too much money too early. And he was trying to build too much. And the company could not adjust to challenges fast enough. Perhaps most important, he didn't listen to his gut. The product was not something that the programmers working on it would use themselves.

CHAPTER 5

Growing Twitter

In late 2006, Williams, Dorsey, and Stone cofounded a new company called Obvious LLC, with Williams as the CEO.

Obvious was a Web product development lab. The goal was to create products fast and at low cost. They would use a small team for each project. Each product would have its own brand. The company would build a network of users as its base. As new products became available, Obvious would introduce them to its network of users. The plan was to use this customer base to encourage market acceptance faster than each product could get by itself.

The goal was to get projects to the point where they were making money from advertising or subscriptions. The money would finance more building. In some cases Obvious would spin off the product into its own company with outside investment. In others, it would offer the product but not develop a separate company for it.

In April 2007, Williams sold Odeo to Sonic Mountain, a privately held New York–based company focused on digital media hosting and search. A month later Odeo won the 2007 Web 2.0 Award for best podcasting site. The award was based on usability, usefulness, social aspects, interface, design, and content quality.

"Web 2.0" is a term that was first used around 2004. It came to refer to Web applications for such "virtual community" uses as social networking, blogs, video sharing, and other services that let the user participate in communication. Beginning in 2005, when it was used as the name of a technology conference, it signaled new interest in the World Wide Web. Enthusiasm for new products and start-up companies in Silicon Valley returned.

THE TWITTER BOOM

Free of Odeo and podcasting, Obvious's founders turned to Twitter. They sought to further develop it as the company's first—and only—project. At the time users were sending several thousand tweets through the Twitter.com Web site daily.

The service was free. So Twitter was not making any money. But Williams, Stone, and Dorsey were intent on building Twitter's value. They knew they had to generate a lot more users. With more users, the company could attract investors to put up the money needed to improve the way Twitter worked.

An opportunity to increase the number of users arose in March 2007 at the SXSW (South by Southwest) annual technology and music conference in Austin, Texas. Twitter workers set up an $11,000, 60-inch (152 cm) plasma television in the conference hallway to demonstrate how Twitter worked.

The techies in attendance jumped all over the idea. They used their cell phones to send text messages. They watched the big screen to see their own messages instantly posted. Soon, attendees found their own uses for Twitter. They tweeted about conference speeches they had attended or planned to attend. They tweeted friends to tell them which bars or restaurants to go to and to agree on places to meet. According to WcP.Watchful.Eye.com, daily Twitter messages shot up from the usual twenty thousand to sixty thousand during the festival.

Valerie Jarrett, later a senior adviser to President Barack Obama, worked as a Chicago-based aide during the 2008 presidential campaign. During the campaign and in the Obama administration, officials used Twitter as a clearinghouse for public statements.

In April, Obvious made Twitter a separate company. Dorsey became CEO. Stone served as creative director.

A second surge in Twitter use occurred in September at the televised 2007 MTV Music Awards. During the broadcast, producers encouraged viewers to tweet comments during the show. Thousands of new users opened Twitter accounts.

FOLLOW ME

Twitter was also gaining attention beyond the world of computer geeks and music lovers. Campaign committees for Democratic senators John Edwards and Barack Obama signed up the year before the 2008 presidential election. They planned to use Twitter, Facebook, and MySpace to reach young voters. The next year, Republican nominee John McCain joined, too.

Candidates used Twitter to advocate their ideas and notify voters about their speaking schedules. Voters used Twitter to share opinions of the candidates and the issues. Twitter use increased during debates between vice presidential candidates Sarah Palin and Joe Biden. There was so much interest in the election that Twitter devoted an entire page of its Web site to political tweets.

Show business celebrities were the next group to come aboard. Fueled by endorsements from such stars as Ashton Kutcher, Lady Gaga, and Elizabeth Taylor, Twitter use continued to grow.

The publicity got the founding trio's phones ringing. First television shows wanted to set up interviews. Then

Overwhelmed and Under Arrest

"Arrested."

That one-word tweet from an American student called his forty-eight followers to act.

On April 10, 2008, James Buck, an American journalism graduate student from the University of California, Berkeley was in Egypt. He was taking pictures of antigovernment protests. Egyptian police picked him up.

Buck's friends in California called the Egyptian consulate there. They asked Egyptian officials to help get Buck released. The friends soon got another tweet:

"Freed."

the founders' pictures began appearing on magazine covers. Cable news networks followed suit. It seemed like everyone—from actors to politicians to newscasters—wanted fans to follow them on Twitter.

Following someone on Twitter is like subscribing to that person's tweets. From the user's Twitter home page, a simple click on "Who To Follow" and "View All" offers a list of potential accounts to follow. The user simply clicks on "+Follow." Tweets from that person

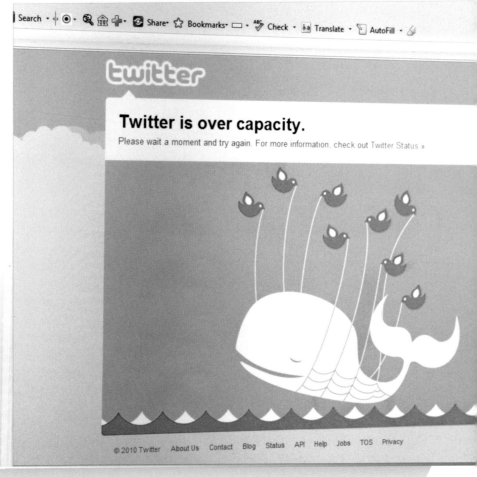

Twitter use grew so fast, Twitter employees had trouble keeping up. At times so many people were tweeting, the site crashed. It displayed a cartoon that came to be known as the Fail Whale.

automatically and immediately arrive in the user's feed. It's just as easy to remove someone from the feed. Just click on "✓Following." The person's tweets no longer come to the home page.

GROWING PAINS

Twitter was ready to seek venture capital. Dorsey took the company through the first two rounds of funding. Kidd, who earlier hired Dorsey at DMSC and partnered with him at dNet, became a first-round investor. After the first round, Dorsey removed his nose ring. He wanted to present an "executive" appearance to the people he was asking for money. The efforts raised $20 million, according to Mediabistro.com.

Twitter was not without criticism. One critic called it a "tool for the shallow and self-centered to broadcast the minutiae of their lives." Another made fun of users who tweeted what they had for breakfast. But most users loved it. Twitter use continued its upswing. The company grew so fast that investors began asking when the founders expected to earn a profit.

The challenge was that usage grew too fast. In the early days, the Web site often crashed. Users complained about seeing the Fail Whale, a cartoon drawing of a whale that told them "Twitter is over capacity." One day in May 2007, the site had an extended period of downtime. Programmers had "a really bad day" when they tried to introduce a new feature that didn't work.

How Did Twitter Grow?

By all accounts, Twitter's growth has been phenomenal. It has demonstrated faster growth than any other social network. Here are the reported figures of registered users from a variety of sources:

Date	Registered users
March 2006	5 (Twitter)
September 2006	5,000
February 2008	450,000
October 2008	3 million
February 2009	7 million
April 2009	20 million
April 2010	106 million
February 2011	175 million
March 2011	200 million

CONFLICT IN THE NEST

With so much happening at once, conflicts arose within the Twitter flock. Founders disagreed on a strategy that included making money. Dorsey had trouble communicating the direction he wanted Twitter to go. But one thing was clear: Dorsey wanted to focus more on improving the amount of time the service stayed in operation and less on creating revenue.

Williams wanted to keep the service free for social users. But he wanted to charge for commercial use. Businesses were using Twitter to their advantage but not paying for it. For example, a Manhattan bakery tweeted when its cookies were done—prompting a flood of customers in the door. But Twitter had no plan for making money. And as of July 2008, no one was even working on one.

Vanity Fair magazine reported that by then, Williams and Dorsey were "barely speaking." Board member Fred Wilson said, "Ev [Williams] and Jack [Dorsey] are a little like John and Paul [Lennon and McCartney]. They made great music together for a while, but then they both kind of got ambitious about things and didn't see eye to eye anymore."

In October 2008, Twitter's board of directors "kicked Dorsey upstairs." They "promoted" him to chairman of the board and replaced him with Williams. Although Dorsey would continue to be involved in strategic decisions, he no longer had a day job at Twitter. Dorsey felt betrayed. He had to watch from the sidelines as others continued work on the service that was his idea in the first place.

@JACK MOVES ON

Dorsey needed a new project. He had just left the CEO job at Twitter and had time on his hands. He learned that his friend and former employer Jim McKelvey had just lost a sale. McKelvey had hired Dorsey back in St. Louis as a summer intern when he was still in high school.

Since then, McKelvey had left the technology industry. He had become an artist and was making and selling hand-blown glass. A potential customer wanted to pay for a piece with a credit card. But McKelvey had no way to accept payment cards. The customer left without making the purchase.

Dorsey learned that many small businesses run into obstacles trying to accept credit and debit cards through such services as Visa, MasterCard, and PayPal. For one thing, the cost was too high. For example, Symbol, a division of Motorola, offers a point-of-sale (POS) wireless credit card terminal. POS means the physical location where goods or services are bought and sold. A POS system is a network of technological devices that provides such services as recording transactions, accepting payment card information, and other tasks.

Motorola's terminal alone cost $900, according to GigaOM.com. That's a lot of money for a small business to pay—especially one with a small number of credit or debit card sales. It's also too high for small businesses that sell lower-priced goods or services.

A SQUARE DEAL

Dorsey got the idea to provide a service that let anyone accept a payment card on a smartphone, iPhone, iPad, or Android mobile device. Users would plug a small, plastic device into their headphone jacks. Users' customers could use it to swipe their cards, verify the amount of the sale, and sign their names.

The company would offer the device and application free. It would charge 2.75 percent of the sale per swipe. By comparison, according to PayPal's Web site in 2011, PayPal charged 30 cents, plus 2.9 percent of the amount of the sale per transaction for payment by debit or credit card.

McKelvey moved from St. Louis to San Francisco. Together Dorsey, McKelvey, and Tristan O'Tierney founded a new company. Dorsey raised $10 million in venture capital, according to GigaOM.com. The company's original name came from something Dorsey saw in the woods when he was camping in California's Marin County near San Francisco. During the night he noticed squirrels scurrying around. They were collecting acorns and

Jack Dorsey demonstrates Square, a device that attaches to a smartphone or mobile device. Customers use it to swipe a credit or debit card to make a purchase.

"squirreling things away." Dorsey saw a connection. His users would be "squirreling" away money. He named the program Squirrel. He envisioned the device shaped like an acorn.

A couple of months later Dorsey was in another company's cafeteria and noticed a squirrel logo. He asked about it and learned that the company was using the name Squirrel Systems for its POS system.

Since Dorsey's project was a POS device, he knew he had to change its name. What worked once could work again. He pulled out a dictionary. He opened it to words that started with "sq." When he came to "square," he stopped. One of the definitions was for "square up." It meant to settle up. That was just what customers do when they pay for goods and services. He changed the name of his device and company to Square.

Square announced its new payment system on December 1, 2009—in a tweet from @square. *TIME* magazine later called it "One of the 50 Best Inventions of 2010."

CHAPTER 6

All the World A-Twitter

Williams took over as Twitter CEO as 2008 came to a close. Its amazing growth continued. It seemed everything Twitter did added new users.

Some ideas for new services came from Twitter's programmers. Others came from users. While Dorsey was CEO, Twitter added permalinks. A permalink (a permanent link) is a Web address (a URL). It's a link to such material as old blog posts after they no longer appear on a site's home page.

They had also added RSS. "RSS" stands for "really simple syndication." Web syndication is making Web content available to multiple other sites. It is especially useful for sites that need frequent updates. RSS makes it easy to publish blogs, news headlines, or other works that change often. Permalinks and RSS expanded the ways people could use Twitter to communicate with each other.

With Williams leading the company, additional services went into production. One was keyword search. It let people see anyone's tweets on a given subject without having to "follow" the person. Twitter also added "reply" and "retweet," or the ability to forward someone else's tweet to others. The company also added "trending topics." That was a list of the top-ten topics people worldwide were tweeting about. All of these new services further increased the number of users.

OUT OF THIS WORLD

As new users signed on, they found new uses for Twitter. One man tweeted in real time while burglars ransacked his home—with him in it! Williams's own wife tweeted during labor and delivery of the couple's son, Miles.

Tweets also involved newsworthy events. On election night in November 2008, President-elect Barack Obama tweeted, "We just made history." Later that month victims tweeted for help during coordinated attacks in Mumbai, India. Terrorists hit a train station, Jewish center, movie theater, hospital, and two hotels.

On January 15, 2009, a passenger on a ferry in the Hudson River snapped a picture of a U.S. Airways jet that had just landed in the water. The event was later called the "miracle on the Hudson." The passenger sent the photo as a tweet. It was the first time a Twitter user beat professional news services to the scene of breaking news.

The "miracle on the Hudson" on January 15, 2009, was the first event communicated via Twitter before traditional news agencies had the story. Since then news items from around the world often first appear as tweets.

In April, Twitter users in Moldova tweeted about violent protests over disputed election results. In June, Iranians used Twitter to publicize riots over election results there. The Iranian government shut down text

messaging. It also barred satellite feeds by news agencies. However, tweets got through to the Twitter Web site. At the request of the U.S. State Department, Twitter postponed a scheduled shutdown for maintenance so that Iranian protesters could keep sending posts. The Iran protests were later called the Twitter Revolution.

The U.S. National Aeronautics and Space Administration (NASA) had been using Twitter for years. NASA used it to tell followers about its schedules and other information. NASA had also relayed messages from astronauts to Twitter accounts. But on January 22, 2010, astronaut Tommy Creamer sent the first live tweet from space: "Hello Twitterverse! We r now LIVE tweeting from the International Space Station—the 1st live tweet from Space! :) More soon, send your ?s."

By March 2010, Stone regularly got calls from news reporters when major events occurred anywhere in the world. (One weakness of Twitter reports, however, is that they are often inaccurate. So are many early reports from professional news crews.)

In February 2009, Twitter ranked third among the most-used social networks, according to Compete.com. In the year between February 2008 and February 2009, the number of Twitter accounts exploded 1,382 percent. It skyrocketed from 475,000 visitors in 2008 to 7 million in 2009, according to Nielsen NetView. Just two months later, the *Wall Street Journal* reported Twitter users had increased again—to twenty million.

When pop music icon Michael Jackson died on June 25, 2009, Twitter processed a record 456 tweets per second as the news spread. Just seconds after midnight (Japan time) on January 1, 2010, Twitter served a record 6,939 tweets.

With so much activity, Twitter needed more workers to keep up. It had only eight employees in January 2008. By April 2009, the *Wall Street Journal* reported Twitter had thirty. The service expected to reach sixty employees by June.

SHOW ME THE MONEY

Twitter was still not making money. Most successful technology start-ups make money either through such activities as sales, subscriptions, or advertising. Or, they sell the company outright. Twitter was an exception.

In April 2009, Williams raised $35 million from investors, according to the *Wall Street Journal*. Williams admitted the company was not making a profit. However, he said, "We want to have as large an impact as possible." That meant the focus was on building use of the service.

So what was Twitter worth? Traditionally, something is worth whatever someone else is willing to pay for it— and the seller is willing to accept. What would others pay for Twitter? In 2009, EncompassSocial.com said Twitter's board of directors had turned down a $500 million offer from Facebook. However, Stone insisted that Twitter was not involved in formal talks. He also said the company was firm. It would stay independent.

In response to questions about whether the service was even for sale, Williams echoed Stone's idea. "The amount of money it would take to buy Twitter right now is

In October 2010, Dick Costolo replaced Evan Williams as Twitter's CEO. He was serious about shifting gears at Twitter to focus on creating a revenue stream and finally show a profit.

more than any company could justify to its shareholders," Williams said.

He added that there were three other possibilities. Twitter could go public, which means it could sell stock to the public. It could stay private and buy out its investors, the way Williams did with Odeo. Or, he said, it could discover some other choice "no one has thought of yet."

While Williams was CEO of Twitter, its online audience snowballed from about three million users to two hundred million, according to the *Washington Times*.

ANOTHER LEADERSHIP CHANGE

In October 2010, Williams stepped down as Twitter's CEO. Speculation was that he was fired, but he insisted that he demoted himself. And no one would say if the board asked him to resign.

Williams stayed on to focus on product strategy. He said the reorganization marked a new phase in Twitter's growth. The company began as a start-up. Now it was ready to shift gears and make some money.

Dick Costolo, who had joined Twitter in 2009 as chief operating officer, became the new CEO. When he joined Twitter, he quickly became known for his sense of humor. He had been an improv comedian in Chicago. At Twitter, Costolo was known as Dick "Keep a da costs a low" Costolo. Stone told *GQ* that Costolo's humor was a big plus. It increased his negotiating skills. It also made simple meetings enjoyable.

Previously, Costolo had founded and acted as CEO of FeedBurner. FeedBurner was a Web feed management service launched in 2004. Google bought it in 2007. Before Twitter, Costolo had also served as a group product manager at Google and manager at Accenture, a management consulting firm. He graduated from the University of Michigan with a bachelor's degree in computer science. He was Twitter's first CEO with a college degree.

SERIOUSLY, SHOW ME THE MONEY

During his first year at Twitter, Costolo led revenue efforts. Williams also gave him credit for "making the trains run on time in the office."

As CEO, Costolo's mission was clear: bring in more money. In December, he brought in new financing to the tune of $200 million, led by venture capital firm Kleiner Perkins Caufield & Byers, according to Reuters news agency.

Costolo also actively sought new advertisers. His efforts began to pay off. *PC Magazine* reported that Twitter sold $45 million worth of ads in 2010. That compared, however, to Facebook's $1.86 billion. The next year, Reuters projected Twitter's ad revenue to reach $150 million. But, according to research firm eMarketer Inc., Facebook was expected to take in about $4 billion in advertising for the same period.

Japan Embraces Twitter

In July 2010, Ev Williams had dinner in Tokyo with five hundred Japanese Twitter fans. Williams was there to celebrate Twitter use among the people of Japan. People in Japan set a world record in June.

Turns out that along with being Twitter fans, the Japanese were huge soccer fans. In a first-round World Cup game, Japan beat Denmark 3 to 1. The Twitterverse in Japan exploded. As the game ended, Japanese fans sent a record 3,283 tweets per second.

In 2010, Twitter estimated that the eight million daily tweets from Japan made up about 12 percent of the total tweets worldwide.

"We make money, but we still spend more money than we make," founder Stone told GQ.com in January 2011. "We do make money via data licensing fees and our new and growing promoted products. But the fact remains, yes, we make money, but we spend more."

According to CIOL, Twitter continued its high user growth. It was adding more than 460,000 new accounts per day. The company also continued to add employees.

GROWTH CONTINUES

For the year 2010, Twitter reported another loss. It had spent the money it took in to increase its business. By comparison, for the same period Google reported revenues of $29 billion and a net income of $8.5 billion, according to Google's investor relations.

But Twitter's future advertising revenues looked promising. Twitter reported that in 2010, 20 percent of tweets mentioned a brand or product. Twitter began selling sponsored tweets. It sold out every available slot.

In February 2011, Twitter had 200 million users sending 130 million tweets per day, according to *eWeek*. And Twitter was still able to attract investors. Andreessen Horowitz invested $80 million in venture capital. At the time, reports estimated Twitter's value at $3.75 billion, according to AllThingsD.com. Just one month later, investors valued the company at more than $7.7 billion, according to Allvoices.com.

Rumors began. Was Twitter for sale? Reportedly both Facebook and Google wanted to buy Twitter. Rumors reported on various blogs said Twitter's board of directors turned down a $2 billion offer from Facebook, as well as a $10 billion offer from Google. Another rumor said that JPMorgan Chase & Company had offered $450 million for a 10 percent share of the company. Founder Stone denied the rumors, saying the reports were "made up." He said there had been discussions with Facebook a couple of years earlier, but Twitter was in no formal talks.

Twitter celebrated its fifth anniversary on March 22, 2011. To celebrate, Stone appeared on *Conan*, Conan O'Brien's show on TBS. O'Brien had previously mocked Twitter as the "Seinfeld of the Internet." He called it a Web site about nothing. However, when NBC fired O'Brien from *The Tonight Show*, he used Twitter to stay in contact with his fans. "It changed my life," O'Brien said.

"We still use you as a great example of how to use Twitter in the best possible way," Stone said.

"Then I should be paid," O'Brien said, to get a laugh.

Back at Twitter's offices, however, not everyone was laughing.

@JACK IS BACK

A week later Dorsey returned. He accepted the job of executive chairman. Raising money was on everyone's mind. Dorsey announced that commercial use of Twitter and its API could lead to paid features. "API" stands for "application programming interface." It is a code that lets software programs "talk" to each other.

Dorsey repeated the three guiding principles he had used when he became CEO in 2007: simplicity, constraint, and craftsmanship. Dorsey's new role was chief of product development.

When Williams learned that Dorsey was coming back, he quit his job at Twitter. He remained, however, a member of the board of directors, as well as a major investor. A few days later Williams told the Huffington Post he was moving on to "explore new business ideas."

The move seemed to confirm reports by CNNMoney.com. Senior writer Jessi Hempel wrote, "There's no shortage of drama at Twitter these days: Besides the CEO shuffles, there are secret board meetings, executive power struggles, a plethora of coaches and consultants, and disgruntled founders."

The *Wall Street Journal* online said that "people familiar with the company" said Williams and Dorsey have had "personal differences." And Dorsey himself, referring to Williams, told *PC Magazine*, "We don't talk."

However, Dorsey also told Financial Markets Regulation Wire that disagreements never have held Twitter back or kept it from growing. "The great thing about any startup and any technology firm is the founders always put the company first," he said.

CHAPTER 7

What's Happening?

Dorsey's return to Twitter—and the departure of cofounder Williams—signaled a new chapter in Twitter's story.

On March 29, 2011, after leaving Twitter, Williams wrote on his blog. "I will venture a prediction about what's next for Twitter," he said. "It will be bigger and better."

Twitter CEO Costolo agreed. He told CNNMoney.com, "We've only achieved 1 percent of what Twitter can be."

In 2011, Twitter was in use in eighty-two countries in seven languages: English, French, German, Italian, Japanese, Korean, and Spanish. Management planned to add more languages that year.

Twitter officials were discussing opening a European headquarters—most likely in London. In fact, they were already hiring representatives in the United Kingdom to tap Europe's advertising market.

The Twitter workforce also changed. Four key, long-time product developers left. But the company hired more than twenty-five new employees. That brought the total workforce to more than 450, according to Mediabistro.com.

Twitter had started April 2007 with a handful of employees. By the following January, there were eight. Ten months later Stone tweeted, "Today we are celebrating our 140th employee at Twitter!" (The company celebrated the number because it equaled the number of characters allowed per tweet.) It took just more than a year to reach the 450 mark. By July 2011, there were five hundred, according to Financial Markets Regulation Wire. But that was just the beginning. In August 2011, Twitter was advertising for more than sixty more employees for support staff, engineers, business development, sales, and other jobs on its recruiting account @JoinTheFlock.

With a new infrastructure in place, Twitter would stay ahead of growth. It also let Twitter launch new products. Engineers improved Twitter's search function. They also added photo sharing and a new tweet button. The simple button gives people with Web sites and blogs an easy way to gain new followers. Most Twitter users have some kind of "follow me" button on their Web sites. But, those buttons simply send visitors to the Twitter Web site to sign up. The new tweet button keeps the visitor on the person's or company's Web site. Pressing the button automatically makes the visitor a follower.

Speculation continued about whether Twitter would be sold. In April 2011, founder Stone told HuffPostTech.com that no one is tempted to sell Twitter. "We have created something that was much bigger and has more potential than we ever imagined," Stone said. The trouble was that the founders had failed to build a business to go with it. They wanted to carry it through to prove they could.

"Once that switch flipped in our heads," he added, "it has become easier and easier to tell people, 'Thank you for your interest, but we are not for sale.'"

Stone also dismissed any thought of taking Twitter public. He said the board of directors was not even discussing the subject.

BUYING BUSINESSES

To improve the way people use Twitter, the company acquired two businesses. TweetDeck and Simply Zesty support Twitter's strategy to add revenue through sponsored tweets and perhaps other forms of product, service, or event promotion.

TweetDeck makes it easy to view, customize, and manage tweets. It also connects users to contacts across Twitter, Facebook, MySpace, LinkedIn, foursquare, Google Buzz, and more. TweetDeck lets users group their followers together. It also lets them divide their Twitter feeds into columns that automatically update. It helps the user organize the massive amount of available information. It's like an automobile dashboard that makes it easy to sort, find, and read tweets and other information. In fact, in techno-speak, it is called a "dashboard."

Twitter's blog said of the purchase, "TweetDeck provides brands, publishers, marketers, and others with a powerful platform to track all the real-time conversations they care about." TechCrunch.com said the price for the London-based company was between $40 million and $50 million in cash and Twitter stock.

TWITTER BUYS SIMPLY ZESTY

Simply Zesty is an online public relations and advertising company. It has offices in Dublin, Ireland, and London. As more businesses use social media to promote their products and services, Simply Zesty helps them create effective campaigns.

With the purchase of TweetDeck, Twitter made it easy for users to view, customize, and manage tweets. TweetDeck also lets users group their followers and connect users to contacts in other social media.

The company offers video production, Web applications, and training. It also offers online monitoring. The service searches social media for mentions of a company's brand and its competitors. It lets businesses know what people are saying about them. Simply Zesty forms a plan to help businesses aim their messages to the right consumers. It also helps businesses in crisis situations if the companies get bad publicity or events put them in the public eye. Simply Zesty creates plans to help clients protect their reputations and effectively communicate.

The purchases of TweetDeck and Simply Zesty indicated Twitter's direction. The two companies offered services useful to businesses. Would Twitter expand its business services? If so, would it offer a premium site that corporate users pay for?

But even as the company focused on raising money, users began to criticize the ads on Twitter's formerly ad-free zone. Part of Dorsey's new role was to pay attention to those critics. He would make sure the original product stayed as useful as possible.

PRIVACY, PLEASE

In March 2011, the Federal Trade Commission (FTC) settled a complaint with Twitter over privacy issues. In January and May 2009, hackers got control of the site. A hacker is a person who breaks into—and often damages—another's computer system. The hackers got access to Twitter users' e-mail addresses, phone numbers, and other nonpublic information. They could view private tweets. They could also send fake tweets that seemed to come from the users.

Who Uses Twitter

The following figures, shown as a percentage of total users, paint an interesting picture of Twitter users:

60	Outside the United States
27	Log in every day
52	Update status every day

Gender

48	Men
52	Women

Age

9	55+
17	45–54
27	35–44
30	26–34
13	18–25
4	13–17

Twitter had told its customers that it was "very concerned about safeguarding" users' information. The FTC said Twitter's security lapses let hackers in and that Twitter put its users' personal information at risk. It also had misled users about how secure the information was. Under the agreement, the agency ordered Twitter not to mislead users about its data protection. The order stands for twenty years. During that time, Twitter also has to put better security in place. The system is to be audited every two years for ten years.

WHAT'S HAPPENING FOR @EV AND @BIZ?

When Williams left Twitter, he reopened the Obvious Corporation he had founded in 2007. At that time, Obvious further developed Twitter and spun it off as its own company. With all the focus and work directed at Twitter, Obvious lay quiet. It ignored additional products or services.

Now Williams was ready to return to the company's original purpose. In global terms, Williams described Obvious as a corporation that "makes systems that help people work together to improve the world." He made a commitment to developing products that matter.

In 2011, Twitter announced plans to move its headquarters from this building at 795 Folsom Street to three floors of an Art Deco landmark at 1355 Market Street, San Francisco, California.

In addition, Obvious would partner with entrepreneurs. It would invest in start-up companies in early to mid-stages. Obvious would help them finance, design, build, and market their company and product. By late summer, the company had already signed its first "Obvious Entrepreneur."

On June 28, 2011, Stone—the founder who had worked at Twitter the longest—announced he was moving on. As founder and investor, he continued to advise Twitter on business strategy. He also planned to continue his work with the Biz and Livia Stone Foundation, as well as schools, nonprofit organizations, and businesses.

A week after Stone left Twitter, Spark Capital, a Boston venture fund, hired him. Spark Capital is a Twitter investor. And one of its partners, Bijan Sabet, serves on Twitter's board of directors. Stone's work at Spark included evaluating investment opportunities.

In late June Stone also announced his return to the Obvious Corporation, which he cofounded. Stone repeated his three-part philosophy of success: positive impact, happiness, and financial reward. In his blog, Stone said that relaunching the Obvious Corporation was "a dream come true."

Another face from Twitter showed up at Obvious. Jason Goldman left Twitter at the same time as Stone. Goldman had been head of product at Twitter. Before that he worked at Blogger and Google. And he was in on the ground floor when Obvious first launched.

WHAT'S HAPPENING FOR @JACK?

Dorsey's return to Twitter was basically a part-time arrangement. Or you could say he had two full-time jobs. He stayed on as CEO of Square, his payment service. The two corporate offices are within walking distance from each other. Dorsey can easily move between them as needed.

In a late June 2011 news release, Square announced it had raised $100 million in financing, led by Kleiner Perkins Caufield & Byers with participation from Tiger Global Management. Kleiner Perkins Caufield & Byers had also invested in Twitter.

At the time, Dorsey's company sold three products: a reader, register, and card case. The Square reader was the device that let users swipe their debit or credit cards through the seller's iPhone, iPad, or Android phones. The Square register was a POS device for the iPad. It accepted payments, tracked inventory, and shared other information. The Square card gave users a way to open accounts at their favorite restaurants or local merchants. It also stored virtual receipts and had a browser.

After developing the first card reader, Dorsey returned to his interest in fashion. Users get a free card reader, but Square also offered a limited-edition "fashionable" version for $10. Fashion designer Vivienne Tam created the Double Happiness card reader. Tam is known for stylish, high-quality clothing with an exotic flair. The limited-edition

Twitter Tools

Twitter's founders valued simplicity and ease of use. They developed some tools to help users effectively use the service.

@ The @ symbol followed by a username is used to mention the person or to reply to his or her tweet.

The # symbol followed by a word or phrase is called a hashtag. Users can group tweets together by topic or type.

D The letter "**D**" followed by a username lets a user send a private message to another user. This is also known as a direct message.

RT To forward someone else's tweet to your followers, click on the word "retweet" under the message. The letters "**RT**" followed by @ and a username means you are forwarding the message from the other user.

> 🔒 The padlock symbol means the user has a private account. Only approved users can follow that person's tweets.

Square device has a red background with contemporary lines suggesting the easy flow of information. Like the free readers, Tam's device plugs into the headphone jack on smartphones and other devices.

Dorsey introduced Tam's device during Fashion Week in 2011. He dedicated $2 from each Double Happiness card reader sold to the Happy Hearts Fund. The nonprofit foundation's mission is to help rebuild children's lives after natural disasters. Its educational programs are available in nine countries. According to its Web site, the Happy Hearts Fund has rebuilt 55 schools serving 34,330 children. Tam sold the reader on her Web site, as well as in retail stores.

WHAT'S HAPPENING WITH THE OTHERS?

Two former Twitter personalities also shared news over Twitter. In March 2011, Noah Glass (@noah), who led the original team that developed the Twitter prototype, tweeted that he was moving back to San Francisco from Los Angeles: "putting life into cardboard. Moving back to San Francisco. Back to life."

And Florian Webber (@csshsh), who worked with Glass and Dorsey on the prototype team, tweeted in April: "In San Francisco. It's been a few years."

The two seeming coincidences may have gone unnoticed if it weren't for a tweet from Dorsey. He sent a picture of himself with Webber to his Twitter followers. The message read: "This is Florian (@csshsh) & me at the @twitter office! Florian was the first Twitter engineer."

In the absence of any formal announcement from Twitter, commentators like Shea Bennett of Mediabistro. com asked, "Has Dorsey decided to put the old team back together?"

Without Williams and Stone, Twitter certainly had room for a couple of innovative employees. Would Glass and Webber return? At the time, no one was talking. But events would soon unfold.

As with all aspects of the Twitter story, future developments would play out over the service that Williams, Stone, and Dorsey created.

Time—and certainly Twitter—would tell.

Fact Sheet on

EVAN WILLIAMS, BIZ STONE, AND JACK DORSEY

Evan Williams: @ev

Birthdate: March 31, 1972

Birthplace: Clarks, Nebraska

Current residence: Berkeley, California

Net worth: $200 million

Marital status: Married to Sara Morishige Williams

Children: One boy, Miles

College attended: University of Nebraska at Lincoln

First job: Freelance copywriter in Key West, Florida

Biz Stone: @biz

Birthdate: March 10, 1974

Birthplace: Boston, Massachusetts

Current residence: Marin County, California

Net worth: $200 million

Marital status: Married to Livia Stone

Colleges attended: Northeastern University; University of Massachusetts Boston

First job: Box mover at Little, Brown and Company

Jack Dorsey: @jack

Birthdate: November 19, 1976

Birthplace: St. Louis, Missouri

Current residence: San Francisco, California

Net worth: $200 million

Marital status: Single

College attended: University of Missouri at Rolla (later renamed the Missouri University of Science and Technology); New York University

First job: Programmer, Mira Digital Publishing

Fact Sheet on

TWITTER

Date first created: March 21, 2006

Company formed: April 2007

Headquarters: 1355 Market Street, San Francisco, CA 94103

Core business: Microblogging service

Number of users: 200 million

Average daily tweets: 140 billion

Number of employees: 500

Languages supported: English, French, German, Italian, Japanese, Korean, and Spanish

Available in: 82 countries

Annual revenue as of December 2010: $150 million

Estimated value July 2011: $10 billion to priceless

Timeline

2000 Jack Dorsey writes program called Stat.us for a portable e-mail device; sends message to five friends from San Francisco's Golden Gate Park.

2004 Ev Williams and Noah Glass found Odeo Inc., the company that develops Twitter as a side project. Biz Stone hired as director of community.

2005 Jack Dorsey hired as a programmer.

June 2005 Apple adds podcasting to iTunes, creating competition for Odeo's developing product. Odeo holds a brainstorming session for new products. Team formed to create prototype.

March 21, 2006 First tweet.

Summer 2006 Williams fires Noah Glass.

September 2006 Williams buys back Odeo from investors.

Late 2006 Williams, Dorsey, and Stone cofound Obvious LLC.

March 2007 SXSW (South by Southwest) annual technology and music conference, Austin, Texas; attendees introduced to Twitter, and thousands sign up.

April 2007 Williams sells Odeo to Sonic Mountain;

Obvious spins off Twitter as a separate company; Dorsey is CEO.

September 9, 2007 Televised MTV Music Awards emcee encourages viewers to tweet their comments.

October 2008 Williams replaces Dorsey as CEO. Dorsey becomes chairman of the board.

November 2008 Barack Obama tweets to thank supporters after winning the U.S. presidential election.

2009 Dick Costolo joins Twitter as chief operating officer.

January 15, 2009 Twitter user breaks news of the "miracle on the Hudson," instead of major news outlets.

April 17, 2009 Actor Ashton Kutcher becomes the first Twitter user to gain one million followers.

May 22, 2009 One billionth tweet

June 25, 2009 Michael Jackson dies; users post a record 456 tweets per second.

December 1, 2009 Dorsey's new venture, Square, announces its new payment system.

January 1, 2010 A record 6,939 tweets are sent seconds after midnight (Japan time).

January 22, 2010 Astronaut Tommy Creamer sends the first live tweet from space.

October 2010 Costolo replaces Williams as CEO; Williams moves to chief of product development.

March 22, 2011 Twitter celebrates its fifth anniversary.

March 29, 2011 Dorsey returns to Twitter as executive chairman and chief of product development; Williams leaves Twitter, stays on board of directors.

April 2011 Noah Glass moves back to San Francisco.

June 28, 2011 Stone leaves Twitter.

Glossary

application programming interface (API) A code that lets software programs communicate with each other.

CD-ROM A compact disk used with a computer that acts as read-only memory; a user cannot change the information on it.

direct message (DM) A private message from one Twitter user to another.

dot-com bubble The period of time between 1995 and 2000 when technology stocks reached record value.

dot-com bust October 9, 2001, when the NASDAQ composite dropped to 1114.11 and lost 78 percent of its value.

follow Sign up to receive tweets from a specific Twitter user; it is like subscribing to that person's tweets.

freelance worker A worker who works for a company without being an official employee; also known as a contract laborer.

hacker A person who breaks into—and often damages—another's computer system.

open source software A free computer program that includes the source code so that people can use it as is or customize it to their own uses.

permalink A permanent link; a Web address where visitors can find such material as old blog posts after they no longer appear on a site's home page.

point of sale (POS) The physical location where goods or services are bought and sold.

POS system A network of technological devices that provides such services as recording transactions, accepting payment card information, and other tasks.

prototype The first working model of a new product or a new version of an older one.

real time Happening now.

ROM Read-only memory; a user cannot change the information.

RSS Really simple syndication; syndication makes Web content available to multiple other sites. RSS makes it easy to publish blogs, news headlines, or other works to multiple sites.

seed money Money for setting up a new business.

short code A unique number, similar to a telephone number, that users can send text messages to.

Silicon Valley A region in Northern California named for the large number of high-tech companies in the area.

source code Text written in a computer programming language.

start-up company A relatively new business still in the research and development stage.

tweet A message of no more than 140 characters sent through a Twitter account.

twitter Chirps of birds, or bursts of trivial information.

URL A string of characters that takes the user to something available on the Internet; a Web address.

vegan A person who eats no fish, meat, chicken, eggs, or milk.

venture capital Money invested in a start-up firm or a small businesses seeking to expand. Investors get part ownership in the company.

Web 2.0 The renewed interest in the Internet after the dot-com crash.

weblog An Internet site—or part of a site—where individuals post regular entries.

For More Information

Association of Information Technology Professionals (AITP)
401 North Michigan Avenue, Suite 2400
Chicago, IL 60611-4267
(800) 224-9371
E-mail: aitp_hq@aitp.org
Web site: http://www.aitp.org
The AITP is a professional development organization for IT professionals. It provides education opportunities for improving technological and business skills, including leadership, networking, peer mentoring, and online resources.

Association for Social Media and Higher Education (ASMH)
George Washington University
2121 I Street NW
Washington, DC 20052
(202) 994-1000
On Twitter: @smhighered
Web site: http://www.socialmediahighered.com
The ASMH brings together social media users, students, and higher-education officials to share information,

learning, tools, and ideas. The association is based at George Washington University.

Biz & Livia Stone Foundation
P.O. Box 66
Corte Madera, CA 94976
Web site: http://www.bizandlivia.org
This fund-raising organization is dedicated to offering grants that help schools, wildlife, and conservation centers.

Canadian Advanced Technology Alliance (CATA)
207 Bank Street, Suite 416
Ottawa, ON K2P 2N2
Canada
(613) 236-6550
E-mail: info@cata.ca
Web site: http://www.cata.ca
The CATA is the largest high-tech association in Canada. It connects businesses across Canada with investors and potential partners worldwide.

Family Online Safety Institute (FOSI)
400 7th Street NW, Suite 306
Washington, DC 20004
Web site: http://www.fosi.org

This organization is dedicated to keeping the Internet safer for children and their families.

International Academy of Digital Arts & Sciences (IADAS)
19 West 21st Street, Suite 602
New York, NY 10010
(212) 675-4890
Web site: http://iadas.net
The IADAS was founded in 1998 to recognize excellence in interactive content across emerging technologies and bring together industry professionals. It also educates members and the public to increase access to new technologies. It also gives Webby Awards for Web sites and individual achievement in technology and creativity.

International Webmasters Association (IWA)
119 E. Union Street, Suite F
Pasadena, CA 91103
(626) 449-3709
Web site: http://www.iwanet.org
The IWA is an international nonprofit association that provides educational and certification standards for Internet professionals. It has more than two hundred thousand members in more than one hundred countries. The organization offers online classes in Web development and e-commerce.

Social Media Club, Inc.

P.O. Box 14881

San Francisco, CA 94144-0881

(415) 692-1002

E-mail: socialmediaclub@gmail.com

Web site: http://socialmediaclub.org

The Social Media Club's mission is "to promote media literacy, promote standard technologies, encourage ethical behavior and share best practices." Its focus is on those who create and consume media: journalists, teachers, students, and toolmakers. It has more than three hundred chapters worldwide.

Society of Internet Professionals (SIP)

120 Carlton Street, Suite 305

Toronto, ON M5A 4K2

Canada

Web site: http://www.sipgroup.org

The SIP is a nonprofit organization for Internet professionals, including programmers, IT personnel, entrepreneurs, and independent experts. Founded in 1997, it upholds professional codes of ethics. It also provides symposiums, panel discussions, and workshops.

Word of Mouth Marketing Association (WOMMA)

65 E. Wacker Place, Suite 500

Chicago, IL 60601

(312) 853-4400

Web site: http://womma.org

The WOMMA is a nonprofit organization that promotes word-of-mouth as a way to solve business challenges. It was founded in 2004 to encourage growth of reliable, ethical, word-of-mouth strategies.

WEB SITES

Due to the changing nature of Internet links, Rosen Publishing has developed an online list of Web sites related to the subject of this book. This site is updated regularly. Please use this link to access the list:

http://www.rosenlinks.com/ibio/twits

For Further Reading

Belcher, Lou. *Ready…Set…Tweet!* Charleston, SC: Lou Belcher, 2010.

Douglas, Nick. *Twitter Wit.* New York, NY: itbooks, 2009.

Fitton, Laura, Michael E. Gruen, and Leslie Poston. *Twitter for Dummies.* Hoboken, NJ: Wiley Publishing, Inc., 2009.

Hay, Deltina. *A Survival Guide to Social Media and Web 2.0 Optimization: Strategies, Tactics, and Tools for Succeeding in the Social Web.* Austin, TX: Dalton Publishing, 2009.

Howard, Tharon. *Design to Thrive: Creating Social Networks and Online Communities That Last.* Burlington, MA: Morgan Kaufmann Publishers, 2010.

Hussey, Tris. *Create Your Own Blog: 6 Easy Projects to Start Blogging Like a Pro.* Indianapolis, IN: Sams Publishing, 2010.

Jones, Monica, and Steve Soho. *Everything Twitter: From Novice to Expert: The Unofficial Guide to Everything Twitter.* Charleston, SC: Create Space, 2009.

Kelsey, Todd. *Social Networking Spaces: From Facebook to Twitter and Everything in Between.* New York, NY: Apress, 2010.

Kirkpatrick, David. *The Facebook Effect: The Inside Story of the Company That Is Connecting the World*. New York, NY: Simon & Schuster, 2011.

LeFever, Lee, and Sachi LeFever. *Social Media in Plain English*. Seattle, WA: Common Craft, 2008.

LeFever, Lee, and Sachi LeFever. *Twitter in Plain English*. Seattle, WA: Common Craft, 2008.

McFedries, Paul. *Twitter Tips, Tricks, and Tweets*. Hoboken, NJ: Wiley Publishing, Inc., 2009.

Mezrick, Ben. *The Accidental Billionaires: The Founding of Facebook: A Tale of Sex, Money, Genius and Betrayal*. New York, NY: Doubleday, 2009.

Micek, Deborah, and Warren Whitlock. *Twitter Revolution*. Las Vegas, NV: Xeno Press, 2009.

Morris, Tee. *All a Twitter: A Personal and Professional Guide to Social Networking with Twitter*. Indianapolis, IN: Que, 2010.

Morris, Tee. *Sams Teach Yourself Twitter in 10 Minutes*. Indianapolis, IN: Que, 2010.

O'Reilly, Tim, and Sarah Milstein. *The Twitter Book*. Sebastopol, CA: O'Reilly Media, Inc., 2009.

Peri, Christopher, and Bess Ho. *Sams Teach Yourself the Twitter API in 24 Hours*. Indianapolis, IN: Que, 2011.

Pogue, David. *The World According to Twitter*. New York, NY: Black Dog & Leventhal Publishers, Inc., 2009.

Qualman, Erik. *Socialnomics: How Social Media Transforms the Way We Live and Do Business.* Hoboken, NJ: WileyPublishing, Inc., 2010.

Safko, Lon. *The Social Media Bible.* Hoboken, NJ: Wiley Publishing, Inc., 2010.

Sagolla, Dom. *140 Characters.* Hoboken, NJ: Wiley Publishing, Inc., 2009.

Stenzel, Pam, and Melissa Nesdahl. *Who's in Your Social Network?: Understanding the Risks Associated with Modern Media and Social Networking and How It Can Impact Your Character and Relationships.* Ventura, CA: Regal Publishing Company, 2012.

Stone, Biz. *Blogging: Genius Strategies for Instant Web Content.* Berkeley, CA: New Riders Press, 2002.

Stone, Biz. *Who Let the Blogs Out?: A Hyperconnected Peek at the World of Weblogs.* New York, NY: St. Martin's Griffin, 2004.

Bibliography

Beattie, Andrew. "Market Crashes: The Dotcom Crash." Investopedia.com, 2001. Retrieved July 28, 2011 (http://www.investopedia.com/features/crashes/crashes8.asp).

Borchers, Callum. "Twitter Co-Founder, Wellesley Native Biz Stone Addresses Babson Graduates." WellesleyPatch.com, May 15, 2011. Retrieved June 6, 2011 (http://wellesley.patch.com/articles/twitter-co-founder-wellesley-native-biz-stone-addresses-babson-graduates).

Bussgang, Jeffrey. "When Jack Dorsey Met Fred Wilson and Other Twitter Tales." TechCrunch.com, April 27, 2010. Retrieved August 16, 2011 (http://techcrunch.com/2010/04/27/jack-dorsey-fred-wilson-twitter-book-excerpt).

Carlson, Nicholas. "Exclusive: An Interview with Twitter's Forgotten Founder, Noah Glass." BusinessInsider.com, April 13, 2011. Retrieved July 5, 2011 (http://www.businessinsider.com/twitter-cofounder-noah-glass-2011-4?op=1).

Carmichael, Evan. "The Twitter Threesome: How Ev Williams, Biz Stone, and Jack Dorsey Got Their Start." EvanCarmichael.com. Retrieved June 10, 2011 (http://www.evancarmichael.com/Famous-Entrepreneurs/5527/The-Twitter-Threesome-How-Ev-Williams-Biz-Stone-and-Jack-Dorsey-Got-Their-Start.html).

Hempel, Jessi. "Trouble @Twitter." CNN Money, April 14, 2011. Retrieved August 27, 2011 (http://tech.fortune.cnn.com/2011/04/14/troubletwitter).

Huffington Post. "HuffPost Celebrates Its 2010 Game Changers with Geoffrey Canada, Sean Penn, Mayor Bloomberg & More." October 29, 2010. Retrieved August 15, 2011 (http://www.huffingtonpost.com/2010/10/29/game-changers-2010_n_775869.html#s168156&title=Jann_Wenner_Arianna).

Jadah. "Christopher Isaac Stone." Bloggermind.net, April 20, 2010. Retrieved June 10,2011 (http://bloggermind.net/christopher-isaac-stone).

Lacy, Sarah. "Evan Williams, Master of the Privacy Game." TechCrunch.com, October18, 2010. Retrieved July 28, 2011 (http://techcrunch.com/2010/10/18/evan-williams-master-of-the-privacy-game).

Liedtke, Michael. "Twitter's Biz Stone Talks Gadgets, Pets, and Sherlock Holmes." Huffington Post, March

31, 2011. Retrieved June 10, 2011 (http://www.huffingtonpost.com/2011/04/01/biz-stone-twitter-interview_n_843497.html).

Malik, Om. "Jack Dorsey on Square, How It Works & Why It Disrupts." Gigaom.com, December 1, 2009. Retrieved August 24, 2011 (http://gigaom.com/2009/12/01/jack-dorsey-on-square-why-it-is-disruptive).

Malone, Michael S. "The Twitter Revolution." *Wall Street Journal*, April 18, 2009. Retrieved June 8, 2011 (http://www.onlinewsj.com/article/SB12400817787330413.html#printMode).

McBride, Sarah. "Twitter Founders Ev and Biz Return to Roots, Relaunch Obvious." Reuters.com, June 29, 2011. Retrieved July 10, 2011 (http://www.reuters.com/article/2011/06/29/us-twitter-idUSTRE75R7AE20110629).

McBride, Sarah, and Alexei Oreskovic. "Twitter Seeking Another Round of Funding." Reuters.com. Retrieved July 5, 2011 (http://www.reuters.com/asets/print?aid=USN1E7641GQ20110705).

McGiboney, Michelle. "Twitter's Tweet Smell Of Success." Nielsen Online, March 18,2009. Retrieved August 26, 2011 (http://blog.nielsen.com/nielsenwire/online_mobile/twitters-tweet-smell-of-success).

Sagolla, Dom. "How Twitter Was Born." 140Characters.com, January 30, 2009. Retrieved June 8, 2011 (http://www.140characters.com/tag/noah-glass).

Smith, Chris, and Marci McGrath. *Jack Dorsey and Twitter*. Greensboro, NC: Morgan Reynolds Publishing, 2011.

Stone, Isaac "Biz." "My Life in Business." GQ.com, January 5, 2011. Retrieved June 8, 2011 (http://www.gq-magazine.co.uk/comment/articles/2011-01/05/gq-column-a-life-in-business-isaac-stone-).

"Twitter Co-founder Jack Dorsey Had Idea at Age 8." Video interview by Vijay Vaitheeswaran, global correspondent. CelebrityNetworth.com. Retrieved August 16, 2011 (http://www.celebritynetworth.com/richest-businessmen/jack-dorsey-net-worth).

Williams, Evan. "The Boss: For Twitter C.E.O., Well-Orchestrated Accidents." *New York Times*, March 8, 2009. Retrieved July 5, 2011 (http://www.nytimes.com/2009/03/08/jobs/08bosses.html).

Index

ABOUT THE AUTHOR

Mary-Lane Kamberg is a professional writer and speaker, as well as co-leader of the Kansas City Writers Group and a member of the Midwest Children's Authors Guild. She is still learning how to use new technology—no smartphone, no iPad, no Kindle.

PHOTO CREDITS

Cover, p. 3 Jemal Countess/WireImage for Time Inc./Getty Images; covers (back and front), multiple interior (blue abstract), multiple interior (red/blue graphic), pp. 58–59 Shutterstock.com; p. 7 © Aurora Photos/Alamy; p. 11 http://en.wikipedia.org/wiki/File:Evan-Williams.jpg; pp. 12–13 © SuperStock/SuperStock; pp. 18–19 © www.istockphoto.com/Günay Mutlu; p. 23 Ethan Miller/Getty Images; pp. 26–27, 64–65, 78–79, 92–93 © AP Images; p. 31 Neilson Barnard/Getty Images; pp. 36–37 © Gamma/ZUMApress.com; p. 38–39 Dawn Majors/MCT/Landov; p. 42 http://en.wikipedia.org/wiki/File:Twttr_sketch-Dorsey-2006.jpg; p. 45 Andrew Harrer/Bloomberg via Getty Images; pp. 52–53 Dan Krauss for the New York Times/Redux; pp. 58–59 © Christin Gilbert/age fotostock/SuperStock; pp. 68–69 © David Robertson/Alamy; p. 74 Jin Lee/Bloomberg via Getty Images; p. 82 Kim White/Bloomberg via Getty Images; pp. 96–97 © Caroline Culler/http://en.wikipedia.org/wiki/File:Twitter_headquarters,_San_Francisco.jpg.

Designer: Brian Garvey; Editor: Bethany Bryan;

Photo Researcher: Amy Feinberg